W9-AHA-703

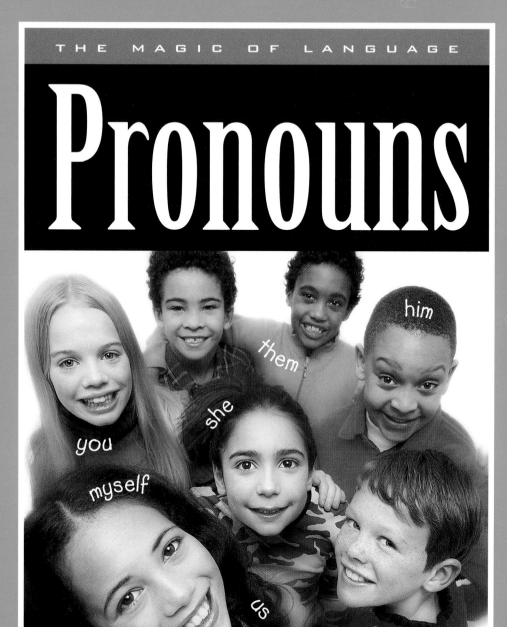

THE MAGIC OF LANGUAGE

Pronouns

By Ann Heinrichs

THE CHILD'S WORLD®
CHANHASSEN, MINNESOTA

Published in the United States of America by The Child's World®
PO Box 326, Chanhassen, MN 55317-0326
800-599-READ
www.childsworld.com

Content Adviser:
Kathy Rzany, M.A.,
Adjunct Professor,
School of Education,
Dominican University,
River Forest, Illinois

Photo Credits: Cover photograph: Punchstock/Digital Vision Interior photographs: Corbis: 12 (J. L. de Zorzi), 20 (Darama), 26; Getty Images/Photographer's Choice/Josef Fankhauser: 23; Getty Images/Taxi: 5 (Gail Shumway), 9 (Lisa Peardon), 11 (Martin Riedl), 24 (Sean Justice); PictureQuest: 15 (Kindra Clineff/Index Stock Imagery), 28 (SuperStock); Punchstock/Digital Vision: 7, 8, 17, 19.

The Child's World®: Mary Berendes, Publishing Director

Editorial Directions, Inc.: E. Russell Primm, Editorial Director; Pam Rosenberg, Project Editor; Melissa McDaniel, Line Editor; Katie Marsico, Assistant Editor; Matt Messbarger, Editorial Assistant; Susan Hindman, Copyeditor; Susan Ashley and Sarah E. De Capua, Proofreaders; Chris Simms and Olivia Nellums, Fact Checkers; Timothy Griffin/IndexServ, Indexer; Cian Loughlin O'Day and Dawn Friedman, Photo Researchers; Linda S. Koutris, Photo Selector

The Design Lab: Kathleen Petelinsek, Design and Page Production; Kari Thornborough, Page Production Assistant

Library of Congress Cataloging-in-Publication Data
Heinrichs, Ann.
  Pronouns / by Ann Heinrichs.
      p. cm. — (The magic of language)
Includes index.
Contents: What is a pronoun?—One or more than one?—What's so special about you?—The three persons—Subject and object pronouns—Whose is it?—You must agree!—Pointing out and asking questions—Indefinite pronouns—When is a pronoun like a mirror?
  ISBN 1-59296-066-9 (library bound : alk. paper)
  1. English language—Pronoun—Juvenile literature. [1. English language—Pronoun.]
I. Title. II. Series: The Magic of Language.
  PE1261.H37 2004
  428.2—dc22   2003020036

TABLE OF CONTENTS

WHAT IS A PRONOUN?

A *pronoun* is a word used in place of a noun.

QUICK FACT

A noun is a naming word. It's the name of a person, place, or thing.

Pronouns help us out a lot.

Without pronouns, we would have to repeat a noun over and over.

Just look at this example:

EXAMPLE

Matthew threw the stick and waited. The dogs ran after the stick, but the dogs couldn't find the stick. Matthew was sure Matthew had thrown the stick near the dogs.

Whew! That's a lot of words! Now look at this example:

*You could say the dogs are playing because the dogs like each other. However, it would be easier to use pronouns. They you'd say **they** are playing because **they** like each other.*

EXAMPLE

Matthew threw the stick and waited. The dogs ran after it, but they couldn't find it. He was sure he had thrown it near them.

Can you see how much easier that is to say? It's easier because we used pronouns to help out.

It, they, he, and **them** are pronouns. They stand in place of the stick, the dogs, and Matthew.

CHAPTER TWO

ONE OR MORE
THAN ONE?

A pronoun can be singular

or plural.

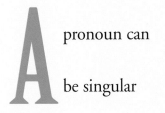

DEFINITION

A pronoun is singular if it refers to just one person or thing.

I, me, he, him,

she, her, and **it** are singular pronouns. They refer to just one

person or thing.

DEFINITION

A pronoun is plural if it refers to more than one person or thing.

We, us, they, and **them** are

plural pronouns. They refer to more than one

person or thing.

Here we are! Look at us! These sentences use the plural pronouns we and us.

CHAPTER THREE

WHAT'S SO SPECIAL ABOUT YOU?

Do you think you are special? Of course **you** are! In fact, all of **you** are special!

RULE

The **pronoun you** can be either singular or plural.

*You are a special person, and **you** is a special pronoun. It can be either singular or plural.*

To talk to everyone on this school bus at once, use the plural pronoun you.

When two friends talk, they call each other **you.** In this case,

you is a singular pronoun. Each friend is talking to just one person.

Suppose Mrs. Martin gets on the school bus. All the children are

standing up or running around. Mrs. Martin needs to count them

before the bus leaves. She says, "Will

you please sit down?"

In this case, **you** is a plural pronoun.

It refers to a whole lot of people. Mrs.

Martin is talking to everyone on the bus.

CHAPTER FOUR

THE THREE PERSONS

A pronoun can be in the first person, second person, or third person.

I am the speaker when I talk about **me.**

We are speaking when we talk about **us.**

I, me, we, and **us** are first-person pronouns.

DEFINITION

A **first-person pronoun** *refers to the speaker.*

There is only one second-person pronoun—**you!** Sometimes your teacher calls on just **one of you.** Sometimes the teacher wants **all of you** to answer at once. **You** is both the singular and plural form.

DEFINITION

A **second-person pronoun** *refers to the person to whom someone is speaking.*

*"How many of **you** want pizza for lunch?"* In this sentence,
***you** is a second-person pronoun and it is plural.*

A **third-person pronoun** *refers to the person or thing about which someone is speaking.*

Here are three chairs. One of them is warmer than the others. Which is it? We use the third-person pronouns them and it when speaking about things instead of people.

If you talk about people, you use **he, him, she, her, they,** or **them.** For birds, trees, and chairs, you use the pronouns **it, they,** or **them.**

He, him, she, her, it, they, and **them** are third-person pronouns. As you see, **they** and **them** can be used for either people or things.

CHAPTER FIVE

SUBJECT AND OBJECT PRONOUNS

As you'll see, the wrong pronoun can sound really silly!

The subject pronouns are **I, you, he, she, it, we, you,** and **they.**

A **subject pronoun** is the person or thing doing an action. It usually comes before the verb, or action word.

EXAMPLE

RIGHT: **She** kicked the ball.
WRONG: Her kicked the ball.

RIGHT: **They** like eating grapes.
WRONG: Them like eating grapes.

RIGHT: **I** feel cheerful today.
WRONG: Me feel cheerful today.

An **object pronoun** is the person or thing receiving an action. It usually comes after the verb, or action word.

The object pronouns are **me, you, him, her, it, us, you,** and **them.**

RIGHT: Maria likes **him.**
WRONG: Maria likes he.

RIGHT: Kevin gave the mouse to **them.**
WRONG: Kevin gave the mouse to they.

RIGHT: Jane baked cookies with **her.**
WRONG: Jane baked cookies with she.

You and **it** can be both subject and object pronouns.

He and I are riding our bikes because bike-riding is fun for him and me.

EXAMPLE

RIGHT: **He** and **I** are riding our bikes.

WRONG: Him and me are riding our bikes.

RIGHT: Give the candy to **her** and **me**.

WRONG: Give the candy to she and I.

WHOSE IS IT?

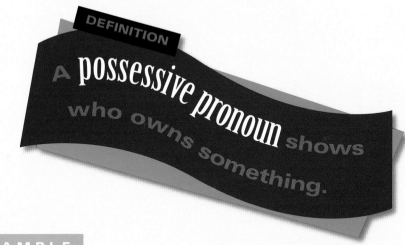

DEFINITION

A possessive pronoun shows who owns something.

EXAMPLE

Give that dog back! It's **mine**!

Take this book. It's **yours.**

Josh has his pen, and Emily has **hers.**

This popcorn belongs to the twins. These pretzels are **theirs,** too.

Mine, yours, hers, and **theirs** are possessive pronouns.

They show who owns the dog, book, pen, and pretzels. Can you name

the owners? The owners are me, you, Emily, and the twins.

Whose dog is this? The answer could be a possessive pronoun. It could be yours or his or ours or theirs.

DID YOU KNOW?

Pronouns are often used before nouns to show who owns something. Examples are my **dog,** your **book,** her **pen, and** their **pretzels. Then those pronouns become possessive adjectives—but that's another story!**

CHAPTER SEVEN

YOU MUST AGREE!

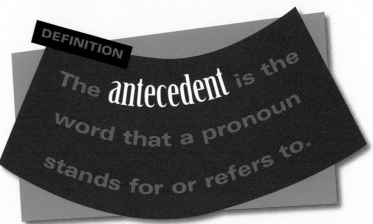

DEFINITION

The **antecedent** is the word that a pronoun stands for or refers to.

Do you remember the definition of a pronoun? It's a word used in place of a noun. That noun—the word that the pronoun stands for—is called the antecedent.

EXAMPLE

Daniel met **Emma. She** is a friendly person.

The **Smiths** just got home. **They** were on vacation.

She refers to the noun **Emma.** So Emma is the antecedent of **she. They** stands for the noun **Smiths.** So **Smiths** is the antecedent of **they.**

Every pronoun *must agree* with its antecedent.

WRONG: If people want to win, you must try harder.

RIGHT: If people want to win, **they** must try harder.

*These **kids** agree that **they** like each other. In this sentence, the pronoun **they** agrees with its antecedent, **kids**. Both are in the third person, and both are plural.*

In this example, **people** is the antecedent. Do you remember the "three persons"? Here we are talking *about* **people,** not *to* the people. So people calls for the third-person pronoun **they.**

*If **Kevin** wants help with his homework, **he** must ask for it nicely.*
*In this sentence, the pronoun **he** agrees with its antecedent, **Kevin**.*

WRONG: If a person wants to win, they must try harder.

RIGHT: If a person wants to win, **he or she** must try harder.

In this example, **person** is the antecedent. Person is singular, so it needs the singular pronouns **he or she.**

HOT TIP

When two singular words are joined by **or,** they act together as a singular idea. In a sentence, a singular verb would be used. When two singular words are joined by **and,** they act as a plural. They take a plural verb.

WATCH OUT!

The antecedent must be clear. Look at this example: "Joe called Tony while he was in town." Who was in town? Joe or Tony? We cannot tell!

It would be better to say: "While Joe was in town, he called Tony" or "While Tony was in town, Joe called him."

CHAPTER EIGHT

POINTING OUT AND ASKING QUESTIONS

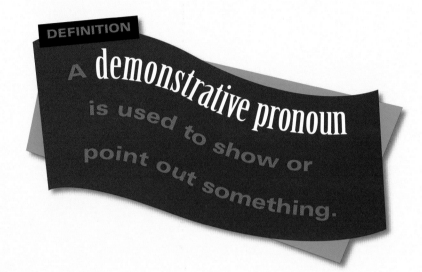

DEFINITION

A *demonstrative pronoun* is used to show or point out something.

This and **these** point out things nearby. **That** and **those** point out things that are farther away. It's easy to imagine your finger pointing when you say these words.

EXAMPLE

This tastes good, but **that** tastes bad.

These are my candies. **Those** are yours.

This is a picture of a boy saying, "Look at *that!*" The demonstrative pronoun *this* points out something nearby. The demonstrative pronoun *that* points out something farther away.

An *interrogative pronoun* is used to ask a question.

Which is my seat? It's hard to tell, but it's easy to know which word is the interrogative pronoun.

HOT TIP

Interrogative pronouns have antecedents, just like other pronouns do. The antecedent is the answer to the question!

EXAMPLE

Who has my backpack?

What is in that sack?

Which is my seat?

CHAPTER NINE

INDEFINITE PRONOUNS

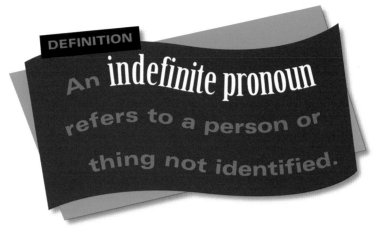

DEFINITION

An **indefinite pronoun** refers to a person or thing not identified.

Suppose Nicole said **something,** and **everybody** laughed.

What did Nicole say? Maybe she told a joke. Maybe she said she wanted a hamburger. Maybe she said she was falling asleep. Whatever she said, that information is not given. So **something** is an indefinite pronoun.

Who laughed? Maybe her friends, family, or classmates laughed. However, the laughing people are not identified. So **everybody** is an indefinite pronoun.

There are lots of indefinite pronouns! Just look: **anyone, anybody, anything, someone, somebody, something, no one, nobody, nothing, everyone, everybody, everything, each, every, either, neither, one, another, much, several, few, both, many, others, all, any, more, most, some, none**

*These two girls are laughing at **themselves**. In this sentence, **themselves** is a reflexive pronoun. It refers back to the subject, **girls**.*

CHAPTER TEN

WHEN IS A PRONOUN LIKE A MIRROR?

DEFINITION

A reflexive pronoun refers back to the subject word.

QUICK FACT

The subject is the person or thing doing the action.

Look into a mirror, and what do you see? You see **yourself.** Well, actually, you see the reflection of yourself. The mirror reflects a perfect picture of yourself back to you.

Suppose a monkey looks into a mirror. Maybe it growls or runs away. Maybe it tries to touch the monkey in the mirror. It sees a reflection of **itself.**

*"I think I will help **myself** to these cookies."* In this sentence, **myself** *is a reflexive pronoun. It refers back to the subject,* **I.**

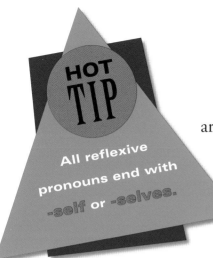

HOT TIP

All reflexive pronouns end with -self or -selves.

Reflexive pronouns work the same way. They are like a mirror. They refer back, or reflect back, to the subject.

The reflexive pronouns are

myself, yourself, himself, herself, itself, ourselves, yourselves, and **themselves.**

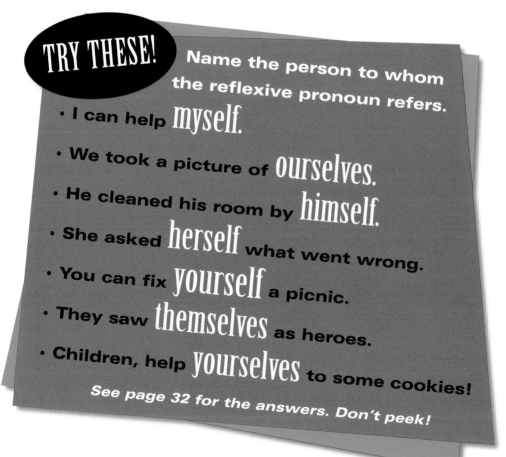

TRY THESE! Name the person to whom the reflexive pronoun refers.

- I can help myself.
- We took a picture of ourselves.
- He cleaned his room by himself.
- She asked herself what went wrong.
- You can fix yourself a picnic.
- They saw themselves as heroes.
- Children, help yourselves to some cookies!

See page 32 for the answers. Don't peek!

How to Learn More

At the Library

Cleary, Brian P., and Brian Gable (illustrator). *I and You and Don't Forget Who: What Is a Pronoun?* Minneapolis: Carolrhoda, 2004.

Collins, S. Harold, and Kathy Kifer (illustrator). *Nouns and Pronouns.* Eugene, Ore.: Garlic Press, 1990.

Heller, Ruth. *Mine, All Mine: A Book about Pronouns.* New York: Puffin Books, 1999.

Terban, Marvin, and Peter Spacek (illustrator). *Checking Your Grammar.* New York: Scholastic, 1994.

Usborne Books. *Nouns and Pronouns.* Tulsa, Okla.: EDC Publications, 1999.

On the Web

Visit our home page for lots of links about grammar:

http://www.childsworld.com/links.html

NOTE TO PARENTS, TEACHERS AND LIBRARIANS: We routinely check our Web links to make sure they're safe, active sites—so encourage your readers to check them out!

Through the Mail or by Phone

To find a Grammar Hotline near you, contact:

THE GRAMMAR HOTLINE DIRECTORY
Tidewater Community College Writing Center
1700 College Crescent
Virginia Beach, VA 23453
Telephone: (757) 822-7170
http://www.tcc.edu/students/resources/writcent/GH/hotlino1/htm

To learn more about grammar, visit the Grammar Lady
online or call her toll free hotline:

THE GRAMMAR LADY
Telephone: (800) 279-9708
www.grammarlady.com

Fun with Pronouns

In this story, think of nouns to replace the boldface pronouns. You can use extra words such as "a," "the," or "and" if you need them. Have a friend do the same exercise. Then compare your stories.

He looked up and saw **it.** It was the color of gold. **She** wanted to bring **it** home, but **he** said it might bite. Soon **they** came along. **She** carefully put a net around **its** body, as **they** watched nervously. **It** didn't wiggle around at all. "Wait till we show **them!**" **she** said. When **they** got home, **he** said, "Look what **we** found!" **They** could hardly believe their eyes. Suddenly **it** began to zoom around the house. **She** said, "Next time you bring **it** home, leave it outside!"

Index

Answers

Answers to Text Exercises

page 29
I
we
he
she
you
they
children

About the Author

Ann Heinrichs was lucky. Every year from grade three through grade eight, she had a big, fat grammar textbook and a grammar workbook. She feels that this prepared her for life. She is now the author of more than 100 books for children and young adults. She has also enjoyed successful careers as a children's book editor and an advertising copywriter. Ann grew up in Fort Smith, Arkansas, and lives in Chicago, Illinois.